C000157484

WEAPON

THE FLINTLOCK MUSKET

STUART REID

Series Editor Martin Pegler

First published in Great Britain in 2016 by Osprey Publishing,
PO Box 883, Oxford, OX1 9PL, UK
PO Box 3985, New York, NY 10185-3985, USA
E-mail: info@ospreypublishing.com

Osprey Publishing, part of Bloomsbury Publishing Plc

© 2016 Osprey Publishing Ltd.

All rights reserved. Apart from any fair dealing for the purpose of
private study, research, criticism or review, as permitted under the
Copyright, Designs and Patents Act, 1988, no part of this
publication may be reproduced, stored in a retrieval system, or
transmitted in any form or by any means, electronic, electrical,
chemical, mechanical, optical, photocopying, recording or
otherwise, without the prior written permission of the copyright
owner. Enquiries should be addressed to the Publishers.

A CIP catalogue record for this book is available from the British
Library

Print ISBN: 978 1 4728 1095 3
PDF ebook ISBN: 978 1 4728 1096 0
ePub ebook ISBN: 978 1 4728 1097 0

Index by Rob Munro
Typeset in Sabon and Univers
Originated by PDQ Media, Bungay, UK
Printed in China through World Print Ltd.

16 17 18 19 20   10 9 8 7 6 5 4 3 2 1

Osprey Publishing supports the Woodland Trust, the UK's leading
woodland conservation charity. Between 2014 and 2018 our
donations are being spent on their Centenary Woods project in
the UK.

www.ospreypublishing.com

The NRA Museums

Since 1935, the NRA Museum collection has become one of the
world's finest museum collections dedicated to firearms. Now
housed in three locations, the NRA Museums offer a glimpse into
the firearms that built our nation, helped forge our freedom, and
captured our imagination. The **National Firearms Museum**,
located at the NRA Headquarters in Fairfax, Virginia, details and
examines the nearly 700-year history of firearms with a special
emphasis on firearms, freedom, and the American experience.
The **National Sporting Arms Museum**, at the Bass Pro Shops in
Springfield, Missouri, explores and exhibits the historical
development of hunting arms in America from the earliest
explorers to modern day, with a focus on hunting, conservation,
and freedom. The **Frank Brownell Museum of the Southwest**, at
the NRA Whittington Center in Raton, NM, is a jewel box
museum with 200 guns that tells the history of the region from
the earliest Native American inhabitants through early Spanish
exploration, the Civil War, and the Old West. For more
information on the NRA Museums and hours, visit www.
NRAmuseums.com.

Author's note

I would like to acknowledge the very kind assistance and advice
of Dr Stephen Bull of the Lancashire Museums Service, as well as
the National Firearms Museums and the Anne S.K. Brown
Military Collection, Brown University Library, Providence, Rhode
Island. Other than as specifically credited, all images are from the
author's collection.

Strictly speaking, the British Army only came into existence
after the Union of 1707, but in practical terms the Scots and
English armies had served as one since the restoration of King
Charles II in 1660. For convenience, therefore, both are referred
to as British irrespective of their actual point of origin.

Editor's note

In this book linear, weight, and volume measurements are given
in imperial units of measurement (yards, feet, inches, pounds,
ounces, grains). Where imperial units of measurement differ from
US customary, the former are used in the text. The following data
will help when converting between imperial and metric
measurements:

1yd = 91.44cm
1ft = 30.48cm
1in = 2.54cm
1lb = 0.45kg
1oz = 28.35g
1 grain = 0.002oz
1 grain = 0.064g

Front cover images: NRA Museums, NRAmuseums.com (top);
Osprey Publishing (bottom).
Title-page image: Claude-Louis-Hector, duc de Villars, is shown
leading French forces at the battle of Denain (24 July 1712) in
this 19th-century work by Jean Alaux (1786–1864) which
provides a surprisingly accurate picture of the uniforms and
equipment of the day. (Public Domain)

Artist's note

Readers may care to note that the original paintings from which
the battlescenes in this book were prepared are available for
private sale. All reproduction copyright whatsoever is retained by
the Publishers. All enquiries should be addressed to:

www.steve-noon.co.uk

The Publishers regret that they can enter into no correspondence
upon this matter.

CONTENTS

INTRODUCTION

The flintlock musket (in British service more commonly known simply as a firelock, or the legendary 'Brown Bess') can fairly claim to be one of the most iconic weapons of all time. It was with flintlock and bayonet that Marlborough and Frederick the Great made their reputations. It was with flintlock and bayonet that Britain, France and Spain contested for control of the North American colonies. Later, it was flintlock-armed Minutemen who first challenged Britain's hard-won hegemony over those colonies at Lexington, Concord and Bunker Hill; and it was French flintlocks which helped facilitate victory in that struggle. Ironically, those same flintlocks which had defeated one empire then went on to create new empires both under Napoleon in Europe, and under the Stars and Stripes in the vastness of the American south-west; and if British ambitions in North America were thereby frustrated, it was the flintlock muskets of the East India Company which won Britain a new empire in the Indian subcontinent and beyond. Ironically, it was in turn the East India Company-designed India Pattern musket which would eventually challenge the Charleville musket of Napoleon's forces in the climactic battle of Waterloo.

As a weapon the musket itself was not new: in its most basic form it can be seamlessly traced back to the medieval 'handgonne'. Seemingly originating in China in the 11th century and making its way to Europe by the 14th century, it comprised a simple iron tube or barrel, sealed at one end. A measured charge of gunpowder was poured down the open end and when ignited through a narrow hole bored through the side of the barrel, the gunpowder charge propelled a lead ball or bullet towards the desired target. In order to flash a flame through the narrow hole and thus fire the weapon, it was necessary first to ignite a small priming charge of gunpowder laid in a shallow pan on the outside of the barrel – hence the terms 'priming pan' and 'touch-hole'. In its earliest form, this priming charge was ignited by literally touching it, first with a heated iron rod and latterly with a burning piece of chemically treated cord or 'slow-match'.

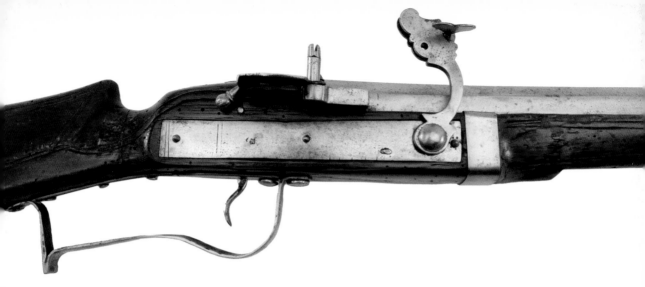

Either could be held in the soldier's hand, but as he obviously needed to look at what he was doing, taking aim while doing so was impossible. Therefore, sometime in the mid-15th century, a simple mechanism or 'lock' was devised to do the job of igniting the priming charge, thus allowing the soldier to squint along the barrel as it did so.

Mechanically, the matchlock was simple and fairly robust, but using it in combat was complicated and to a degree compromised by the separate elements that needed to be brought together. In the first place the soldier had to carry around with him a length of slow-burning match-cord. This was served out in the same proportions as the rest of his ammunition: 1lb of powder, 1lb of lead shot and 1lb weight of slow-match. The inconvenience of having to carry around 1lb of slow-match was made all the more so because inevitably a considerable proportion of a soldier's time is spent waiting, and during that time an equally prodigious amount of match-cord might be consumed to no purpose – but if it were not kept lit, precious time might be lost in lighting it when it was needed. Slow-match was also temperamental. It was susceptible to damp, not just in falling rain which was liable to extinguish it entirely, but in 'damnifying' it so that although it might be smouldering, the burning ember might not actually be hot enough to ignite the gunpowder. Even under optimal conditions the loading process required the match to be detached from the musket, then reset in the clamp in the right place to ensure that the glowing end would descend precisely into the priming pan. If, of course, the soldier was kept waiting for any time, the match would need to be constantly adjusted as it burned down. Not surprisingly, accidents were common, it being all too easy for the soldier to forget that he was carrying a lighted match in the presence of gunpowder. Even without those complications there were tactical drawbacks in that the smoke (and the smell of it), and at night the glow of the match, rendered concealment or a stealthy approach difficult.

The solution was the firelock, so called because by striking a flint against a steel or frizzen, the lock or mechanism reliably created its own fire to ignite the powder – and did so only as and when required. The

This Spanish firearm of the late 16th or early 17th century is an absolutely typical example of the matchlock musket, and is identical to those illustrated by Jacob de Gheyn II (1565–1629) that appear later in this book. Both its simplicity and its limitations are immediately apparent. In order to make it ready for firing, after the main charge of powder and ball had been loaded via the muzzle of the barrel, the pan over in the centre had to be opened and a priming charge of powder sprinkled into the pan. The pan cover was then closed again while a slow-burning match-cord was fixed into the curved pan and its setting checked by lowering it gently towards the pan. If satisfied, the soldier would then adopt a firing position, flick open the pan cover again and on the word of command pull the trigger to bring the burning match down on the exposed priming charge. (NRA Museums, NRAmuseums.com)

Dating from 1813, this watercolour shows an Austrian infantryman (identified by his single-breasted white jacket and double-peaked shako) engaged in bayonet practice with a fur-capped French grenadier. By this period bayonet fencing was being widely cultivated as a skill in its own right, and this appears to be a preliminary sketch for one of the many broadsheets which appeared, illustrating sequences of the various individual thrusts and guards specially developed by fencing masters. Their actual utility in what was necessarily a brutal business without rules is perhaps questionable. Nevertheless, the colourful broadsheets were very popular and normally depicted the duellists, whether fighting with bayonets or with swords, in the uniforms of opposing armies – with the soldier finally receiving the fatal thrust invariably being an enemy soldier. (Anne S.K. Brown Military Collection, Brown University Library)

weapon could now be loaded in advance, sometimes a long time in advance. It could be carried in a variety of ways over all kinds of terrain, and in adverse weather conditions, in daylight or in the dark, and then made ready to fire in a matter of seconds. Moreover, once it had been fired it could be reloaded and fired again quickly and easily, and a bayonet could be fitted to it for close-quarter fighting.

The importance of this development cannot be overstated, for it was not simply a matter of the technical improvement of an existing weapon, the musket, but in effect the creation of an entirely new firearm. In the wars of the 16th and 17th centuries the musket had proved to be an increasingly important weapon, but at the same time it was just one component in a complex military machine which featured a variety of specialist weapon systems. For much of the period the pikeman was regarded as the more important arm, and the musketeer's role initially was no more than to provide fire support for the assault or the defence against it. Over time that role grew in importance and the numbers of musketeers grew accordingly, so that by the latter stages of the English and French civil wars in the 1640s most infantry – and in some engagements all of them – were armed with muskets. Nevertheless, the technical limitations of the matchlock still precluded the musket from realizing its full potential.

That changed with the adoption of the firelock or flintlock, which not only overcame those limitations but exponentially exceeded them with the addition of the bayonet, thus making each musketeer his own pikeman. The military revolution which began with the introduction of gunpowder was complete, for almost inadvertently the flintlock musket had created the universal soldier.

slightly earlier, some genius realized that if the pan cover were to be hinged forwards rather than sideways and the steel or frizzen attached to the rear of the pan cover at a 90-degree angle (or thereabouts), the flint would not only strike upon it but simultaneously throw it forwards, thus opening the pan to receive the resultant shower of sparks.

This development, known as a Snaplock or Snapwark and sometimes later variously identified as a Baltic Lock or an English Lock, was again much simpler, albeit surprisingly crude in appearance. However, while comparatively more reliable, an unfortunate deficiency remained in the design. In theory, when cocked the weapon would only fire if the trigger was squeezed to disengage the sear from the tumbler. Alas, not only were negligent discharges common, but jolting or dropping the weapon could also see it fire of its own accord, especially if the manufacturing tolerances were sloppy. What was required was some kind of safety device.

The first solution was the addition of a 'back-ketch', or 'dog', which clipped into a notch in the rear of the cock and prevented it going forward unless manually disengaged. Initially, weapons so fitted were sometimes known as 'half-bent' locks, since it was literally half-bent or half-cocked after loading. This allowed the pan to be primed and the cover to be closed over it, while the dog was then automatically disengaged by fully drawing back the cock as and when the user was actually ready to fire the weapon. This safety catch worked reasonably well, and the dog-lock was therefore used for both military and hunting weapons well into the 18th century.

By then, however, it had been superseded by the invention of the fundamentally similar but simpler and more reliable fusil (from the Italian *fucile* or flint), which is credited to a multi-talented gentleman named Marin le Bourgeoys. Born into a noted family of artisans in Normandy in about 1550, Bourgeoys attained a degree of fame as an artist, inventor and gunsmith. In 1598 he was appointed a *valet de chamber* (royal servant), and by 1608 he had a workshop in the Louvre Palace. There he was employed, among various other duties, in making high-quality firearms both for the king's own use and as gifts for favoured courtiers and foreign princes and dignitaries. In so doing he not only refined the quality of the pieces he made, but the actual mechanisms as well, and sometime between 1610 and 1615 he completed the evolution of the flintlock into what would be its classic form.

The internal arrangement of the lock was simplified, and by cutting a second and rather deeper notch in the tumbler below the first Bourgeoys created a secure half-cocked position, removing the requirement for an external safety catch. This invention gave French military muskets a pre-eminence they never lost – a point underscored by the fact that Bourgeoys' lock was simply known as the French Lock. In due course the French Lock was universally adopted throughout Europe; and having cleaned up the original rather cluttered prototype, work was undertaken to improve the lock's appearance. The rather crude and ugly pan cover and steel assumed a more aesthetically pleasing rounded shape, while the equally crude S-shaped cock gave way to a more elegant swan-shaped style – but this eventually proved to be insufficiently robust for military use and had to be reinforced with a ring set into the neck.

Internally, there were to be some functional improvements too, but these were largely minor in nature. The most important improvement was the introduction of a 'bridle' in the 1680s. This was a small bridging plate first attached over the tumbler and then extended to cover the sear. This did not alter the functionality of the lock in any way but provided a bearing for the otherwise unsupported end of the tumbler axle, thus rendering the lock more robust and less susceptible to 'getting out of order'. Similarly, an external bridle was extended forward from the priming pan to support the screwed axle of the steel, and by the mid-18th century this had evolved into a double bridle centring the priming-pan cover. Inserting a roller in the end of the arm or peg bearing on the frizzen spring made for a smoother operation. A gently dished priming pan ensured that the priming charge drained towards the touch-hole; and there were even attempts to render the priming pan waterproof which included a sliding cover for the touch-hole, although few such innovations found their way into military use. However, all of these alterations and improvements, successful or otherwise, were merely refinements, and in its final form the flintlock mechanism was still very similar to that perfected by Marin le Bourgeoys in the Louvre Palace at the beginning of the 17th century.

DIVERGENT DEVELOPMENT

As to the weapon itself, most muskets for the French Army were produced at three arsenals. In 1665 an adviser to the Parliament of Paris, Maximilien Titon de Villegenon, seigneur d'Ognon, assumed responsibility for maintaining a stockpile of weapons for the king's troops at the *Magazin Royal* housed in the Bastille. Initially, there was no official specification or pattern beyond the calibre and barrel length, and manufacture was contracted out to gunmakers at Saint-Étienne and other traditional areas. With the French Army almost continuously at war over the next 50 years, it then became necessary to establish two Royal factories – Charleville and Maubeuge in 1678 – while weapons for the Ministry of Marine largely came from a factory established in 1691 at Tulle, near Liége. Most weapons, however, continued to come from private individuals or entrepreneurs.

A similar process was followed in England, where the Board of Ordnance based at the Tower of London was primarily a receiver rather than a manufacturer of muskets other than by the setting up of components. For the most part the manufacture of muskets was contracted out to independent gunmakers in London and latterly in Birmingham as well, who in turn subcontracted or pieced out the individual components all the way down to screws and sidenails. The completed arms, or sometimes just the components, were then delivered to the Board of Ordnance at the Tower of London, which was responsible for placing the orders and for carrying out proof-testing and other quality-control checks upon delivery.

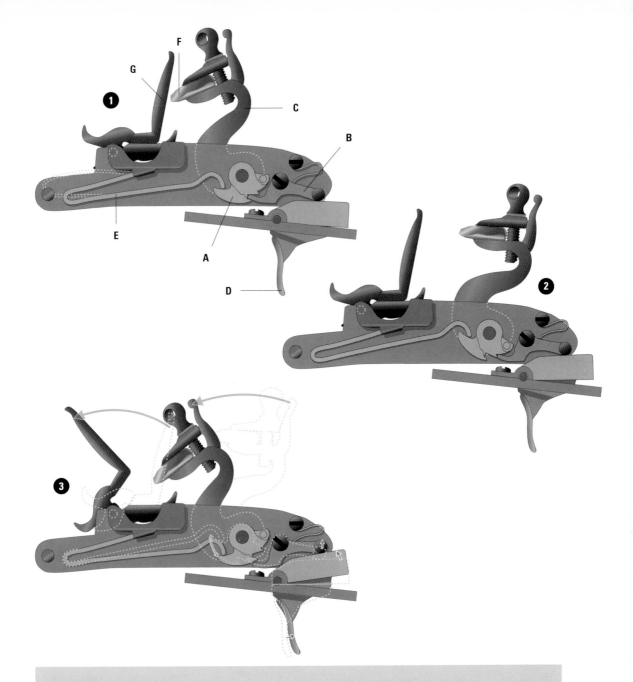

The flintlock mechanism

The half-cock position (**1**) was used for carrying and handling loaded muskets. For the sake of clarity the bridle, which would otherwise obscure the tumbler (**A**), has been omitted. Note how the sear (**B**) is engaged in the lower, rebated, slot at the bottom of the tumbler, very effectively locking it in place. To fire, the cock (**C**) was drawn back into the fully cocked position (**2**); the tumbler fixed to it was slightly rotated in a clockwise direction so that the sear was now engaging the upper slot, which was not rebated. Upward pressure on the sear by the

trigger (**D**) would thus release the tumbler. With the tumbler released the powerful mainspring (**E**) pressed it down, rotating the cock forward (**3**) so that the flint (**F**) struck and threw forward the frizzen (**G**), creating at the same time a shower of sparks to ignite the powder in the priming pan.

In normal circumstances ignition was swift and sure, but there was then usually a slight delay between the firing of the priming charge and the main one in the barrel. It was this delay which the Revd Alexander Forsyth would successfully obviate by means of his percussion system.

13

The Land Pattern adopted in 1722 formed the basis for all subsequent British Army muskets up to the adoption of the Pattern 1853 Enfield. This particular example (above) from the Museum of Lancashire in Preston bears the signature of R. Watkin, a gunmaker active between 1710 and 1740, and like an identical piece in private hands has a 36in barrel rather than the 46in barrel of the Land Pattern, although the three ramrod pipes are positioned at the correct distances for the latter, suggesting that at some point in time the barrel was cut down in length, perhaps for use by light infantry. This particular weapon and its twin have the initials 'YC' stamped in the stock, which are conjectured to stand for York Castle. The heavy piece of brass furniture (below), known as the sideplate, housed the sidenails; these were large screws which passed transversely through the stock to secure the lock. (Lancashire Museums)

Both systems ensured a basic level of commonality – at least in terms of calibre and barrel length – but there was still scope for variation between manufacturers. However, after half a century of near-continuous warfare ended with the Peace of Utrecht in 1713, the French and British governments, in 1717 and 1722 respectively, took the opportunity to introduce a greater degree of standardization by laying down sealed or official patterns.

The form of the musket, as established by these patterns, followed two divergent paths. The barrel was set in a trough cut out of the top of the wooden stock, and originally secured by transverse pins passing though both the stock and metal loops brazed to the underside of the barrel. From at least 1716 onwards, however, external bands of iron or brass began to replace the pins on French muskets. This change offered a number of advantages in that the musket could be taken apart more easily for cleaning and repair and was also significantly lighter. The French Modèle 1777, for example, weighed 9.9lb while its direct British equivalent, the Short Land Pattern, although 2in shorter, weighed in at 10.5lb. Redesignated as the Modèle 1777 corrigé en l'an IX, or An IX for short, this particular musket not only served as the standard firearm

of Napoleon's army, but was also cloned for most German armies during the Napoleonic Wars (1803–15) and by the United States as the Model 1812/1816 Springfield.

Significant numbers of the Modèle 1777, originally ordered by the French Government, were even manufactured by British contractors in the 1790s and instead issued to Allied troops and auxiliary units. Otherwise all British flintlock muskets continued to follow the older

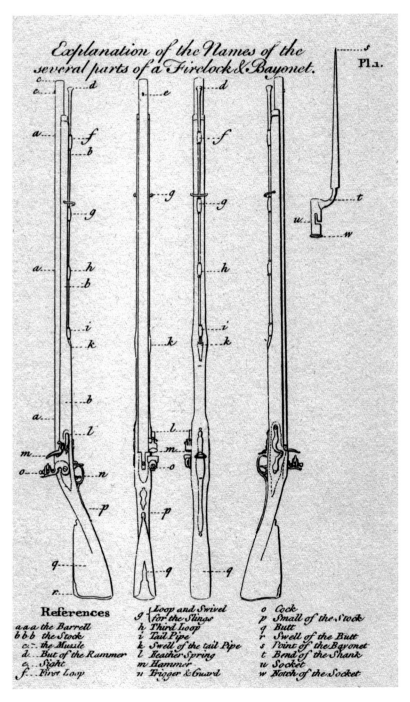

Explanation of the Names of the several parts of a Firelock & Bayonet.

Pl.1.

References

a a a the Barrell
b b b the Stock
c .. the Muzzle
d .. But of the Rammer
e .. Sight
f .. First Loop

g { Loop and Swivel { for the Slings
h Third Loop
i Tail Pipe
k Swell of the tail Pipe
l Feather Spring
m Hammer
n Trigger & Guard

o Cock
p Small of the Stock
q Butt
r Swell of the Butt
s Point of the Bayonet
t Bend of the Shank
u Socket
w Notch of the Socket

A contemporary explanatory drawing naming the parts of the 18th-century British Army flintlock musket, seemingly first published in William Windham's influential *A Plan of Discipline, Composed for the Use of the Militia of the County of Norfolk* (London, 1759). Notwithstanding the association with militia, the weapon used as a pattern appears to be the regular Army issue Land Pattern, popularly known as the Brown Bess. The origin of the term is obscure and Victorian suggestions that it was a reference to Good Queen Bess (Elizabeth I of England) are fanciful. Most likely it derives from the German *Büchse* or gun and dates from the Continental wars against Louis XIV of France in the 1690s and early 1700s, when flintlock muskets finally replaced matchlocks. The term was certainly in use by way of British soldiers' slang in the 18th century, much as more modern soldiers still refer to their rifle by the old Anglo-Indian slang term 'bundhook' – or at least still did in the author's day.

styling, with pins securing the barrel to a heavier and sturdier stock. In fact, it was not until the adoption of the Pattern 1853 Enfield rifle-musket that the switch was made to the use of external bands.

It should be emphasized that the dates of adoption in the accompanying table relate only to when a particular model was first approved, rather than when it was actually taken into service with front-line units. For a fortunate few this might have occurred quite quickly, but as a general rule of thumb the service life of a musket was reckoned, in the British Army at least, to be about 12 years, and new muskets would normally only be issued as and when required. A particular case in point is the New Land Pattern musket. This was approved in the spring of 1802, but production had barely begun when it was temporarily halted in May 1803 upon the renewed outbreak of war with France. Some 20,000 examples of the light-infantry variant were ordered to be set up in 1811 for eventual issue to those regiments so designated, but only the Foot Guards and the 4th Regiment of Foot had received the ordinary version before Waterloo! Consequently, the British Army actually fought its way through the Napoleonic Wars with the existing Short Land Pattern and India Pattern muskets, rather than with the more modern 1802 New Land Pattern. Conversely, the India Pattern had originally been set up for the East India Company as long ago as 1771; it was routinely issued to British regular troops serving there long before the first Government purchases in 1793 and thereafter survived in service long enough to be converted into a percussion weapon in the 1840s.

The Short Land Pattern differed from the earlier, original Land Pattern in having a slightly more refined lock and a shorter barrel. Officially the barrel was 42in long, but this example (below) from the Museum of Lancashire has a barrel length of 38in. There were at least three generations of the Whateley family engaged in various aspects of the Birmingham gun trade up until the 1790s, and the crown and cypher mark indicates that this weapon was set up to a government contract. The escutcheon plate (below right) set into the neck of the stock primarily served as an anchor point for a transverse screw securing the rear of the trigger-guard – necessary because of the strain imposed on it by the rear sling-swivel. It was also an obvious location for engraved decoration or badges. In this instance it appears to identify a Lancashire Volunteer unit of 1798. (Lancashire Museums)

BRITISH, FRENCH AND AMERICAN MUSKET VARIANTS

The principal variants of British, French and American military smooth-bored flintlocks are set out in the table below. The table is obviously far from comprehensive, and excludes rifled weapons of all kinds and minor variants, together with specialized classes such as the Sea Service muskets produced for Britain's Royal Navy and also a confusing variety of regimental-pattern cavalry carbines. However, for the sake of comparison it does include a representative sample of those pattern flintlocks used by certain other countries.

DESIGNATION	COUNTRY	ADOPTED	CALIBRE	BARREL LENGTH	TOTAL LENGTH
Modèle 1716 (Marine contract)	France	1716	.69	47in	62.5in
Modèle 1717	France	1717	.69	46in	62in
(Long) Land Pattern	Britain	1722	.75	46in	62in
Short Land Pattern (Dragoons)	Britain	1722	.75	42in	58in
Ordinäre Flinte	Austria	1722	.72	46in	62in
M1723	Prussia	1723	.72	45in	60in
Modèle 1728	France	1728	.69	46in	62in
Modèle 1729 (Marine contract)	France	1729	.69	44.5in	61in
M1740	Prussia	1740	.72	41.25in	56.5in
M1752	Spain	1752	.69	41in	57.5in
Ordinäre Commiss-Flinte	Austria	1754	.72	44in	59.5in
Light Dragoon carbine	Britain	1756	.68	36in	52in
Artillery carbine	Britain	1757	.68	42in	58in
Militia Pattern	Britain	1757	.75	42in	58in
Modèle 1763	France	1763	.69	44in	60in
Modèle 1763 (cavalry)	France	1763	.69	34in	50in
Short Land Pattern (infantry)	Britain	1768	.75	42in	58in
East India Company contract	Britain	1771	.75	39in	55in
Elliot carbine (Light Dragoons)	Britain	1773	.66	28in	43.5in
Modèle 1777	France	1777	.69	44in	60in
Modèle 1777 (Artillery)	France	1777	.69	36in	51in
Modèle 1777 (Dragoons)	France	1777	.69	42in	57in
Modèle 1777 carbine	France	1777	.69	30in	45in
Model 1795 (Springfield)*	USA	1795	.69	44in	60in
Model 1795 (Harpers Ferry)	USA	1801	.69	42in	58in
Heavy Dragoon carbine	Britain	1796	.75	26in	42in
India Pattern (Army)**	Britain	1797	.75	39in	55in
New Land Pattern	Britain	1802	.75	42in	58in
New Land Pattern (Light Infantry)	Britain	1803	.75	39in	55in
M1809	Prussia	1809	.72	41.25	56.5in
Paget carbine (light cavalry)	Britain	1812	.66	16in	31.5in
Model 1816 (Springfield)***	USA	1816	.69	42in	58in

*A copy of the French Modèle 1763.

**This was exactly the same weapon first set up for the East India Company in 1771 and which continued to be manufactured until 1839.

***A copy of the French Modèle 1777.

The India Pattern was based on the Land Pattern series, but had a 39in barrel and simplified furniture. This particular example has a lock marked up to Ketland & Co., active in Birmingham from *c.*1809 (formerly William Ketland of Steelhouse Lane), and was probably manufactured around that date as it still has the older swan-neck cock. This would appear to be a hybrid private-contract weapon, perhaps for a local militia unit, as it does not bear a crown and cypher and has the 42in barrel of the Short Land Pattern. Note the brass forend cap (left) protecting the end of the stock and the 'trumpet'-shaped ramrod pipe (at the muzzle end only) accommodating the iron ramrod. Note also the stud brazed on top of the barrel, not primarily as a front sight but a means of securing the bayonet. (Lancashire Museums)

CALIBRE

When first introduced in the latter part of the 16th century the musket was distinguished from other military firearms not only by its longer barrel, but also by its calibre, which was at first of 12 bore; i.e. 12 spherical bullets of the appropriate size could be cast from the 1lb weight of lead which, together with the 1lb of gunpowder and 1lb of slow-match, represented the usual ammunition scale of the day. Not surprisingly this, together with a long barrel, resulted in a comparatively heavy weapon, typically weighing some 14lb, which normally required a *fourchette*, or forked staff, upon which to rest it when firing.

In the French service, by the second half of the 17th century, the smaller and lighter 14 bore or .69 calibre was preferred since it did not require the use of a rest, and for convenience the same calibre was also used for cavalry weapons and other specialist variants. This happy standardization was in marked contrast to British service, where the calibre remained the same but the barrel length was reduced from 54in to 48in in 1628 and then to 46in by 1722 for infantry muskets. Having established that calibre for infantry muskets, there remained a rather confusing multiplicity of calibres for other weapons. Throughout most of the 18th century, for example, ordinary regiments of British dragoons, still being regarded as mounted infantry, carried .75-calibre infantry muskets, distinguished only by a very slightly shorter barrel. Indeed, it was largely exactly the same weapon which was adopted by the British infantry in 1768 as the Short Land Pattern. In 1796 it was

Flintlock ammunition

Gunpowder or black powder is a mixture of sulphur, saltpetre (ammonium nitrate) and charcoal. In general terms, the efficiency of the gunpowder is determined by the strength of the saltpetre and the degree to which it is adulterated with charcoal. Ideally it should comprise 75 per cent saltpetre, 15 per cent charcoal and 10 per cent sulphur, but this mix was not always achieved.

Sulphur is a naturally occurring substance almost exclusively found in volcanic regions. In Europe production was largely centred in Sicily, but in the 18th century Britain was able to import significant quantities through the agency of its increasingly important East India Company. Similarly, Britain also enjoyed virtually unlimited access to cheap, good-quality saltpetre from India. British gunpowder was therefore consistently admired as being very good indeed. The supply of saltpetre in France, on the other hand, was much less certain and required the licensing of contractors to dig it from below outhouses and stables – an unpopular process that was often destructive of the buildings concerned. The quantity and quality suffered accordingly and as a result, French gunpowder was not only reckoned less powerful but produced more residues with which to clog both barrel and mechanism. The establishment of a Gunpowder Commission in 1775 went some way to alleviating this, but more effective still was the devising of an artificial process (first seen in Prussia) called Putrefaction, which quite literally involved the decomposition of animal and vegetable matter by a process of fermentation in what were termed *nitrières* or *salpêtrières*.

Charcoal (usually willow charcoal) was the easiest and cheapest of the three ingredients to obtain, and consequently there was sometimes a tendency to adulterate gunpowder with too much of it. Mexican gunpowder encountered during the Texas Revolution in 1835–36 and the US–Mexican War in 1846–48 was judged to be very poor stuff and dismissed by one Texian observer as 'little better than pounded charcoal' (quoted in Hardin 1994: 34).

In gunpowder's earliest form, each of the three ingredients was ground to a dust or flour-like consistency before mixing. Known as Serpentine powder, this suffered from two crucial weaknesses. First, it did not travel well and there was a marked tendency for the different ingredients to separate out. This could be rectified to a degree by stirring it all together again immediately before use, but a greater problem was that the density of the fine powder and the resultant lack of oxygen inhibited combustion. The solution to both problems was to bind together the ingredients first with water and later with distilled spirits to form a paste which was then compressed, dried and finally 'corned' in a mill to produce consistently sized granules.

Propelled by 70 grains (4.5g) of good-quality powder, the .71 soft lead ball was a potent man-stopper with the potential to shatter large bones. All too often, however, that lethal potential fell away dramatically if the powder was damp or of poor quality; instead of a penetrating wound a contusion was a more common outcome, and a 'spent' ball might even bounce off thick clothing. 'Double-shotting' a weapon – i.e. stuffing two balls rather than one into the barrel – could obviously increase the lethality, but due to the time required in doing so this was only practical before going into battle. Otherwise, the only significant ammunition variants were the use of 'small shot' or buckshot in the manner of a shotgun, although this was rarely issued as a military round, unlike the peculiarly American practice of using the so-called 'buck and ball round'. The latter, as the name suggests, was a round of ammunition combining an ordinary musket ball with three or four buckshot. In either case the buckshot did little to increase the initial lethality of the round, but it obviously complicated the wound and increased the likelihood of infection.

LEFT A 'pebble', or flint, is shown alongside original .71 balls for British Land Pattern muskets of .75 calibre. This shard of quartz, usually measuring about 0.75–1.2in square, was knapped or shaped by striking flakes off to create a wedge shape with a sharp cutting edge which would strike sparks off hardened surfaces such as steel. Without it, the flintlock musket was useless.

replaced by a much handier short-barrelled carbine, but the calibre remained the same: .75. Other British cavalry also carried short carbines; sometimes of individual regimental patterns and of varying barrel lengths, but this time usually – though not invariably – in .65 calibre.

However, carbines were by no means restricted to cavalry use. While the term is now exclusively applied to short-barrelled weapons, it could also be used at the time to denote almost any small-calibre firearm irrespective of barrel length. In 1758, for example, a carbine was issued to a variety of light-infantry and Highland regiments and independent companies. At first glance there was nothing to distinguish this carbine from an ordinary infantry or dragoon musket, for it had a 42in barrel. However, not only was it of a smaller .68 calibre (effectively the same as the French Army musket), but it weighed only 7.75lb, in contrast to the 10.5lb of the similarly dimensioned Short Land Pattern. At various times similar carbines were also set up for sergeants and cadets, but in recognition of the potential for confusion, they were often designated as fusils.

As if the multiplicity of calibres was not confusing enough, most musket balls were actually cast smaller than the notional calibre of the musket in order to ensure that they could easily roll into the barrel, even if it was heavily fouled. Consequently, British muskets with a calibre of .75 in fact fired a .71 ball. There was a decided (if not entirely warranted) feeling amongst some British commentators that their heavier .71-calibre bullet gave them an edge over the French in combat. As long ago as the battle of Malplaquet (11 September 1709), for instance, Captain Robert Parker opined after a firefight between the Royal Irish Regiment and the Royal Regiment of Ireland in the French service that: 'The advantage on our side will be easily accounted for, first from the weight of our ball; for the *French* Arms carry bullets of 24 to the pound; wheras [*sic*] our *British* Firelocks carry ball of 16 only to the pound, which will make a considerable difference in the execution' (Parker 1968: 88–89). In reality, the difference between the individual rounds probably had rather more to do with the quality of the gunpowder used than the slight difference in the weight of the ball.

MUSKET ACCESSORIES

Accoutrements

Until late in the 17th century, musketeers carried pre-measured charges of gunpowder in a series of wooden or tin bottles suspended from a leather bandolier. Ideally, the number of bottles or 'boxes' corresponded to the calibre of the weapon. Thus the original 12-bore muskets required 12 bottles or boxes of powder for the 12 bullets carried separately in a small bag or even in the soldier's pockets, plus an additional box for priming powder. However, more or less coincidentally with the widespread introduction of the flintlock, the pre-packed paper cartridge began to replace the inconvenient bandolier. As early as 1644 an English writer named John Vernon described in *The Young Horseman* how

> if you use Cartrages, you shall finde in your Carttreg case a turned wooden pin which you must take, having cut lengths of white paper something broader then the pin is in length, and rowle the paper on the pin, then twist one end of the paper, and file it almost full of powder, then put the bullet on top of the powder, twisting that end also. (Vernon 1644: 10)

Vernon's book was aimed at cavalrymen, as its title suggests, but infantry too were soon using such cartridges. In either event, the introduction of cartridges was a staged process in which, at first, the powder and bullets were still carried separately, but eventually both were combined in a single package – albeit, in the case of the French Army, not until as late as 1720.

The adoption of cartridges greatly simplified the provision, transportation and carrying of small-arms ammunition. As early as the mid-1640s, musketeers in the English Royalist army were being issued with 'powder bags' rather than bandoliers. No illustrations survive, but as they were furnished with a girdle or waist-belt they were presumably not unlike the French *gargousier* or belly box. A quantity of cartouche or cartridge boxes of tin covered in leather were certainly ordered for the New-Modelled Parliamentarian Army in 1645, and a 1662 order for the Battle-Axe Guards of Ireland specified that theirs were to be 'Tyn Cartouch boxes covered with Leather of Calves Skin for Muskets with Formers, pryming boxes and neate [ox] leather girdles' (quoted in Blackmore 1994: 30).

The capacity of these belly boxes was obviously quite limited, and in the French service at least the paper cartridges were supplemented by a largish *poire à poudre*, or powder flask, made of leather or horn. This was slung on the right hip together with the ball bag and a small priming flask. It was not until about 1730 that this arrangement was replaced on the hip by the more familiar *giberne*, or cartridge box. Similarly, in Britain, adoption of a proper cartridge box had come much earlier, but again the capacity of the box had been surprisingly limited, requiring it to be supplemented by expedients such as a belly box worn on a belt around the waist or by a tin 'magazine' clipped to the sling. In the end the cartridge box itself was enlarged. The wooden block was replaced by tin compartments and the capacity (for British ones at least) increased to as much as 60 rounds.

Even then, battlefield resupply was sometimes necessary. In the early days powder was transported in bulk by the barrel, and resupply during an engagement required a soldier to scoop loose powder from the barrel into his empty chargers. This was a process fraught with danger as several soldiers jostled together at the same time, and if one of them in his haste forgot that he was carrying a lighted slow-match, the result could be unfortunate. Cartridges, on the other hand, could be packed in barrels or boxes for transportation and then delivered straight to the firing line using improvised carrying parties. After the campaign in Flanders in 1794, one British officer recorded:

French infantry equipment, 1697. (B) is the belt; (C) is the buckle; (D) is the bayonet frog; (E) is the socket bayonet; (F) is the priming flask; (G) is the picker, for cleaning out the touch-hole; (H) is the bullet bag; (I) is the protective flap; and (K) is the powder flask or *poire à poudre*.

It would be doing a great injustice to the women of the army not to mention with what alacrity they contributed all the assistance in their power to the soldiers while engaged, some fetching their aprons full of cartridges from the ammunition wagons, and filling the pouches of the soldiers, at the hazard of their own lives, while others with a canteen filled with spirit and water, would hold it up to the mouths of the soldiers, half choked with gunpowder and thirst … (Quoted in Lawson 1961 III:107)

Just how widespread this particular expedient might have been is difficult to say, although it was clearly managed with the active co-operation of the quartermaster sergeants, and similar stories come from both the French and American armies.

Whether the cartridges or packets of cartridges were carried up to the firing line by soldiers detailed for the purpose or by non-combatants such as soldiers' wives, the essential point is that the near-simultaneous adoption of the flintlock musket and the paper cartridge meant that the soldier not only had a simple, robust weapon which could be fired more quickly, more reliably and more effectively than before, but also a new type of ammunition which could support that increased firepower.

Bayonets

In addition, the soldier also had a bayonet. The term apparently dates back to at least the latter part of the 16th century and was originally applied to a type of long-bladed hunting knife or dagger, similar to the German *Hirschfänger* and seemingly made in the French city of Bayonne, near the foot of the Pyrenees. As firearms came to supersede the more traditional crossbow for hunting, the utility of jamming the *bayonette* into the muzzle to convert the musket instantly into a boar-spear soon became apparent. The process by which this hunting weapon became a military one is easily explained.

As noted earlier, in the early 17th century matchlocks accounted for the overwhelming majority of military muskets, with the technically more complicated and expensive flintlock largely restricted to specialist companies of 'Firelocks'. These small units sometimes had a semi-ceremonial role as lifeguard or bodyguard units attached to a particular officer, e.g. Prince Rupert's Firelocks during the early part of the English Civil War (1642–51), or the Battle-Axe Guards of Ireland, or alternatively they might be employed to guard the artillery train. However, other companies were used as scouts and skirmishers and quite naturally, like 18th-century German *Jäger*, these were often recruited from among foresters, gamekeepers and huntsmen. Equally naturally, those recruited in the Pyrenean foothills for the French Army brought their bayonets with them, and the practice soon spread. As the various companies and eventually whole regiments of men armed with firelocks were not mixed with pikemen, there was a clear need for some means of defending themselves against direct assault, especially by cavalry, and the bayonet readily presented the answer.

A grenadier of Britain's Coldstream Guards is a little uncertainly depicted in this watercolour by C.J. Lyall (1845–1920). Supposedly representing a soldier at the time of their introduction into the regiment in 1670, the uniform depicted probably dates from about ten years later. As was customary at the time, as a grenadier this man's coat is extravagantly decorated with loops and tassels, and the once practical nature of the forage cap, which later evolved into the famous mitre cap, can easily be appreciated. Of most interest, however, is the plug bayonet. Although depicted over-scale, its origin as a dagger, complete with cross-guard, is readily apparent. Examples exist of flintlock muskets with slightly belled muzzles, opened out specifically for the purpose of accommodating plug bayonets. Needless to say, such muskets could only be altered to accommodate the later socket bayonets by shortening the barrel in order to remove the belled muzzle entirely. (Anne S.K. Brown Military Collection, Brown University Library)

Both these bayonets are British; the upper one was made by John Gill in Birmingham sometime between 1805 and 1817, and the lower one by J. or Wm. Makin in London between 1800 and 1820. Note how the triangular blade is not only offset from the socket slotting on to the muzzle in order to allow the musket to be fired while the bayonet is fixed, but is also angled away to make reloading the musket easier. The mortised socket, although simple, was far from secure, and a variety of locking devices were devised. In the case of the lower example, the collar has been removed, probably sometime after October 1844, and replaced by another, now lost, that was adapted to fit a spring catch underneath the barrel of the musket.

The earliest reference to such weapons in the British service appears to come in March 1663, when included amongst the equipment back-loaded after the abandonment of Dunkirk were 500 'short swords or Byonetts' (quoted in Blackmore 1994: 31). The use to which they had been put is not clear, and they may indeed have been in store there when the English took over the place five years earlier. Whatever the explanation, bayonets were certainly issued to a regiment of fusiliers raised in France in 1671 and to a regiment of dragoons raised in England in the following year, while the Royal Regiment of Fusiliers had them when first raised in 1685. The significance in all three cases is that the rank and file in question were all armed with flintlocks. At much the same time, grenadier companies were being added to ordinary infantry regiments and they, too, had flintlocks and bayonets.

All of these early bayonets were still of the plug type, jammed into the muzzle of the musket; indeed, for a time some muskets were made with slightly flared barrels the better to accommodate them. While no-one doubted the utility of the bayonet, there was an obvious problem in that once the barrel was plugged the musket could not be fired. A variety of solutions were attempted, generally using rings to attach the bayonet to the side of the barrel, but in the 1690s the first socket bayonets were introduced. The handle was replaced by an iron tube, attached to the blade by a cranked shaft, which slipped over the end of the barrel. In order to accommodate and secure the tube, the wooden stock was shortened accordingly and a substantial stud or lug brazed to the barrel just short of the muzzle. A mortised slot cut out of the tube then engaged with the lug to secure it on to the barrel. By 1702, the French Army was equipped with socket bayonets. The British Board of Ordnance purchased huge numbers of plug bayonets between 1689 and 1703, and no mention is made of socket bayonets until an order placed in August 1703.

The musket could now be loaded and fired with the bayonet fixed, at which point it was realized that the balance of the musket was adversely affected. This particular issue was partially addressed by altering the shape of the blade – replacing the original flat dagger with a lighter triangular spike with deep fullers in the two outer faces, while the inner face was angled away from the muzzle to facilitate reloading. Triangular blades appeared on plug bayonets of the late 17th century, but were not adopted by Britain until c.1715; their superior strength was well known from their use on smallswords of the period.

Not surprisingly, there were a number of variations on this basic pattern over the life of the flintlock musket, the most bizarre being the kukri-bladed version carried by some early Gurkha units in the 1820s and 1830s. Fundamentally, however, except for the addition of a variety of locking devices, this basic form eventually carried the bayonet long beyond the life of the flintlock.

Slings

One further and easily overlooked accessory remains to be described in brief – the carrying sling. The first reference to it appears to come in Johann Jacobi von Wallhausen's *Kriegskunst zu Pferd* of 1616, in which mounted dragoons are depicted with muskets slung on their backs. Significantly, the sling resurfaced in the second half of the century with the advent of the hand grenade, used in the siege warfare which then dominated military operations in Europe. As with the early dragoons, the sling was required in order for the musket to be carried on the soldier's back while leaving both hands free. Although the tossing of hand grenades soon went out of fashion the sling did not, and the tanned- or buff-leather strap became a standard attachment to all flintlock muskets. Notwithstanding its simplicity, it was a significant development which enhanced the individual soldier's versatility, allowing him to march further and faster, especially in difficult terrain, and was thus the final link in the process by which the flintlock musket created the universal soldier.

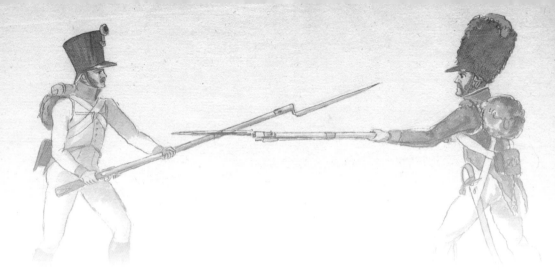

USE
The search for a tactical doctrine

SUPPLANTING THE PIKE AND MATCHLOCK

At the time of the flintlock musket's introduction, most infantry regiments were still combined-arms units, comprising both musketeers *and* pikemen. Of the two the 'puissant pike' was originally regarded as the more important arm, whether in attack or defence, but by the 17th century its status was sharply in decline in relation to the matchlock musket. As late as the 1650s the official ratio in most European armies was two musketeers to each pikeman, but in practice the true proportion of musketeers was generally much higher. It was becoming increasingly difficult to recruit and more importantly retain pikemen, far less persuade them to wear the necessary armour. 'Cabinet practitioners', or armchair theorists, were still

This splendid detail from a hand-coloured etching by Romeyn de Hooghe (*c.*1645–1708) depicts a rather fanciful scene purporting to represent the siege of Londonderry by King James II's forces in 1688–89. Although generic in nature, it nevertheless provides a very useful illustration of infantrymen in action during the transitional period when the matchlock musket was in the process of being supplanted by the flintlock and the pike was being replaced by both. Note the way in which the musketeers are still leaning well forward, as in the days when the musket was fired supported by a staff or *fourchette* and how, notwithstanding there being very few pikes, the cavalry are returning fire with their flintlock pistols and carbines rather than attempting to charge home with their swords. (Anne S.K. Brown Military Collection, Brown University Library)

Musketeers of the late 16th century, by the Dutch artist Jacob de Gheyn II. Note the excessive clutter of equipment required to service the heavy matchlock musket, including the staff or *fourchette* required to rest it on when firing. (Anne S.K. Brown Military Collection, Brown University Library)

Then again, the comparatively long barrel of the infantry flintlock might at first sight seem to be awkward for loading, but when doing so the musket was generally angled so that the muzzle was only a little more than chest-high. Moreover, the manual exercise, or weapon-handling drill, first introduced by Prince Johan of Nassau in the 16th century was a means not just of teaching a soldier how to carry, load and fire his musket; through constant practice of that exercise it was also intended to inculcate an easy dexterity in handling the weapon. In 1607, the Dutch artist Jacob de Gheyn II had created a superb set of engravings illustrating Nassau's manual exercise, and subsequently a long line of other artists depicted successive variations and improvements well into the 19th century. The artistic quality rarely matched that of Jacob de Gheyn II's original engravings, but what all of them had in common was that they more or less meticulously depicted each individual step of the process.

To load the flintlock musket it was first necessary to balance it in the left hand, half-cock it and open the priming pan with the right hand, and then take out a cartridge. This was bitten open and a small quantity of powder sprinkled into the pan, which was then closed and the musket 'cast about' and held on the left side at such an angle as to lower the muzzle to chest height, this being convenient to pour the remainder of the powder down the barrel and stuff the ball and cartridge paper after it. The paper normally served as wadding and helped reduce windage, i.e. the gap between the diameter of the ball and the internal diameter of the barrel.

Ordinarily, the ramrod was used to tamp down the charge solidly; but soldiers proceeding on sentry or other duties requiring loaded weapons, though with no certainty of firing them, would load a 'running ball' – that is, simply drop the ball down the barrel without any wadding or ramming of the charge, so that when coming off duty they could unload the weapon simply by upending it. Similarly, a widely used expedient in combat was to strike the butt end on the ground and rely on the weight of the ball to

Drilling with the flintlock musket

This sequence of photographs illustrates the British *Manual Exercise 1764* as used during the American Revolutionary War (1775–83) and afterwards. Obviously, there were variations from army to army and over time, but none were of any real substance, and this 35-stage sequence is entirely typical.

In the 'Position of a soldier under arms' (**1**) the soldier was enjoined to 'stand straight and firm upon his legs; Head turned to the Right; Heels close; Toes a little turned out; the Belly drawn in a little, but without constraint; the breast a little projected; Shoulders square to the front, and kept back; the right Hand hanging straight down the side, with the Palm close to the thigh; the left elbow not to be turned out from the body; the firelock to be carried on the left Shoulder, as low down as can be admitted without constraint; the three last Fingers under the Butt; the fore Finger and thumb before the Swell; the Flat of the Butt to be supported against the hip-bone, and to be pressed so that the firelock may be felt against the left side, and that it may stand before the Hollow of the Shoulder, not leaning towards the head nor from it; the barrel almost perpendicular.'

'I. Poise your Firelocks!' (**2**): the soldier grasps the neck of the stock with his right hand and holds it up directly in front. The left hand initially slaps against the swell of the stock. In 'II. Cock your Firelocks!' (**3**), the left hand now holds the stock while the right hand cocks the weapon. This is followed by 'III. Present!' (**4**) and 'IV. Fire!': note how the soldier's weight is placed on his left foot, while the musket itself is supported at the swell of the stock.

'V. Half Cock your firelocks!' (**5**) is followed by 'VI. Handle your Cartridge!' (**6**) and then 'VII. Prime!' (**7**); the cartridge is bitten open and a small quantity of powder is sprinkled into the priming pan. Then 'VIII. Shut your Pans!': the soldier is instructed to 'shut your pan briskly, drawing the right arm at this Motion towards your Body, holding the Cartridge fast in your Hand … Turn the Piece nimbly round to the loading position, with the Lock to the Front, and the Muzzle the Height of the chin, bringing the right hand behind the muzzle; both feet kept fast in this Motion'. 'IX. Charge with Cartridge!' (**8**) is followed by 'X. Draw your Rammers!' (**9**) and 'XI. Ram down your Cartridge!' (**10**). The next step is 'XII. Return your

Rammers!' (**11**): the soldier is commanded to 'Return the rammer, bringing up the piece with the left hand to the shoulder, seizing it with the right hand under the cock, keeping the left hand fast at the swell, turning the Body square to the Front'.

'XIII. Shoulder your Firelocks!' (**12**) is the 'under arms' position. This is followed by 'XIV. Rest your Firelocks!' (**13**) and then 'XV. Order your Firelocks!' (**14**), with 'XVI. Ground your Firelocks!', 'XVII. Take up your Firelocks!', 'XVIII. Rest your Firelocks!' and 'XIX. Shoulder your Firelocks!' after that. 'XX. Secure your Firelocks!' (**15**) is the posture adopted in heavy rain or other adverse weather in order to keep the lock dry within the soldier's armpit and prevent rainwater running down the barrel. For the same reason, the sling-swivels were so positioned that when slung, the musket would be carried with the butt up and muzzle down. It is followed by 'XXI. Shoulder your Firelocks!'

'XXII. Fix your Bayonets!' (**16**) is followed by 'XXIII. Shoulder your Firelocks!' and then 'XXIV. Present your Arms!' (**17**): this is the saluting posture. (A somewhat similar posture was adopted by the French infantry in advancing with the bayonet.) The next step is

'XXV. To the right Face!' followed by 'XXVI. To the Right Face!' and then 'XXVII. To the Right about Face!'. 'XXVIII. To the Left Face!' (**18**) is followed by 'XXIX. To the left Face!', 'XXX. To the left about Face!' and 'XXXI. Shoulder your Firelocks!'

'XXXII. Charge your Bayonets!' (**19**) sees the soldier instructed to 'Bring the Swell of the Firelock down strong upon the palm of the hand, turning upon both heels to the right, the right Hand grasping the Piece at the Small behind the Lock, and as high as the waist-belt: the firelock upon a level with the Barrel upwards'. It is followed by 'XXXIII. Shoulder your Firelocks!' in which the soldier is required to 'Bring the Firelock to the Shoulder, place the left hand upon the Butt, bringing the feet square to the Front'. In 'XXXIV. Advance your Arms!' (**20**) the soldier is ordered to 'Bring the Firelock down the right Side with the right Hand, as low as it will admit without Constraint, flipping up the left Hand at the same Time to the Swell, the Guard between the Thumb and fore Finger of the right Hand, the three last fingers under the cock, with the barrel to the rear'. It is followed by 'XXXV. Shoulder your Firelocks!'.

self-tamp it. In either event, at that point the musket was brought back to the shoulder, or directly to the 'recover' – held vertically in anticipation of the order to open fire.

As to the time required for the loading process, it is important to appreciate that those meticulously detailed illustrations of the manual exercise were intended for instructional purposes only. In basic training each and every individual step of the exercise was necessarily the subject of a separate spoken command. However, once the recruit had mastered the process it was speeded up considerably and the ponderous individual commands were replaced by just three: 'Make Ready!', which encompassed the whole of the loading process, including if necessary the locking of ranks; 'Present!', at which point the soldier cocked his musket and levelled it at the enemy; and 'Fire!' or 'Tirez!' (Pull!), as the case might be.

Following the widespread introduction of the iron ramrod in the 1730s, constant practice in this manual exercise could achieve a theoretical rate of fire of as many as four to five rounds a minute. Just as today, however, loading and firing too quickly was counter-productive and increased the natural tendency to fire high. Indeed, the all-too-common business of raw or over-excited troops 'shooting at the skies' was to be a constant theme throughout the life of the musket, from its very earliest days all the way up to the American Civil War (1861–65) and beyond. If anything, the effect of such wild (and consequently harmless) firing was to encourage rather than dismay those being shot at. Consequently, far from urging haste, officers were enjoined to steady and if necessary *slow* their men's rate of fire, ensuring in particular that they took the time to level their pieces properly before pulling the trigger.

2me feuille d'exercice de la charge en douze temps et dix huit mouvements, apparently intended as a very basic primer in the manual exercise – i.e. the loading and firing of the musket – during the French Revolutionary Wars (1792–1802). A startling variety of uniforms are depicted, and although most wear the 'National' uniform of a blue coat with red and white facings, the two figures wearing helmets may be wearing the old pre-Revolutionary *chasseur* or light-infantry uniform. Two others wearing a form of shako may also be intended as *tirailleurs* or sharpshooters, but it is equally possible that they are intended to represent volunteers of the Polish Legion. (Anne S.K. Brown Military Collection, Brown University Library)

Reliability

For the most part the flintlock was normally very reliable, and on pulling the trigger the soldier could reasonably expect it to fire. There were, nevertheless, a number of factors which could adversely affect that reliability, beginning with the flint, which might simply fail to strike sufficient sparks to ignite the priming charge. There were various reasons for this, not the least of which was the fact that the flint itself might be defective. It was generally held, for example, that while British gunpowder was accounted the best in the world, British flints were reckoned much inferior to French ones, and consequently they were often disparagingly referred to as 'pebbles'. Even if the flint was of good quality and properly 'knapped', or shaped, it would soon become blunted in use and require to be replaced after 10–15 firings.

The flintlock could also be adversely affected by the fact that black powder is extremely hygroscopic and will happily absorb moisture from the atmosphere. Unfortunately, even moderately damp powder, especially if of poor quality in the first place, will prove reluctant to ignite, and soon clog the barrel, touch-hole and priming pan, thus necessitating constant scouring to clear them. The problem became immeasurably more difficult, of course, when the flintlock was exposed to direct rainfall. Although the priming pan was normally accounted shower-proof, both flint and frizzen were less likely to produce the required shower of sparks if slicked by rain. However, at the battle of Culloden, after a blustery morning on 16 April 1746, Private Edward Linn reckoned that the Jacobites 'thought it was such a bad day that our firelocks would not fire, but scarce one in our regiment missed firing, but kept them dry with our coat laps' (quoted in Tomasson & Buist 1962: 175). Once an initial shot had been discharged, the barrel could generally be kept sufficiently warm and dry through constant firing, but heavy rain – especially if prolonged – was a different matter. Famously, at the battle of Fishing Creek on 19 January 1862, Confederate infantrymen, finding their flintlock muskets useless in the heavy rain, not only threw them away but smashed them against trees and fences to ensure they would not be gathered up and reissued. It should be emphasized, however, that this action was exceptional and related not just to the adverse weather but to the age of the weapons themselves.

During the 18th century the British Army reckoned, as a general rule of thumb, that the flintlock musket had a maximum useful life of about 12 years. This was far exceeded, however, by those weapons which performed so dismally at Fishing Creek, and scarcely less so by those carried by the Mexican Army in the 1840s. Over time, not only was there a tendency for the lock mechanism to become worn, sloppy and sometimes downright dangerous, but corrosion led to the touch-hole in the barrel opening out, thus leading to an alarming blow-back effect. Not only did this inhibit the soldier himself from holding the weapon anywhere near his face, but it also tended to scorch the man standing next to him. The understandable result was a pronounced tendency to fire the weapon from the hip, abandoning any pretence of taking aim. Nevertheless, in criticizing the behaviour of Mexican troops for doing so in the 1840s (and anyone else armed with rusty and worn-out cast-offs) it is extremely important to recognize that much of the supposed inadequacy of the flintlock derived from the lamentable condition of weapons purchased 20 or more years before, rather than any intrinsic defect in design.

Performance

While an individual musket ball might carry a good deal further, the absolute maximum useful range of the flintlock was generally held to be no more than about 300yd and in reality a good deal less. In 1755, for example, two companies of supposedly very highly trained Prussian grenadiers shot at a target 10 paces (8.33yd) broad and 10ft high, hitting it with 46 per cent of rounds fired at 150 paces (125yd) and 12.5 per cent of rounds fired at 300 paces (250yd). Similarly, a series of tests carried out in Britain by a King's German Legion officer named William Muller (or Mueller) about 50 years later recorded the percentages of hits scored by musket-armed soldiers against a comparable target. At 100yd, 40–53 per cent hits were achieved; at 200yd, this fell to 18–32 per cent; and at 300yd, only 15–23 per cent hits were recorded. In each case, the lower figure was seemingly achieved by 'ordinary soldiers' firing volleys on the word of command and the higher figure by 'well trained men'. In both the Prussian and British tests the 10ft-high target can hardly be regarded as realistic, even though Muller declared his version to represent a body of cavalry. Very few men are 6ft tall – let alone 10ft tall – and given the well-attested propensity of musket-armed soldiers to shoot high at the best of times, an uncomfortably high percentage of these hits would actually have gone over the heads of an enemy infantry company.

In France, on the other hand, Ernest Picard recorded only very slightly different results in 1800 against a smaller and more realistic target measuring just 5.75ft tall by 3.3yd wide. At 75m (82yd), 60 per cent hits were recorded; at 150m (164yd), 40 per cent hit the target; at 225m (246yd) the hit rate fell to only 25 per cent; and at 300m (328yd), 20 per cent. At even closer ranges the performance improved dramatically. In an informal modern test, utilizing upended wooden railway sleepers as targets, it was actually found to be difficult to *miss* at 25yd – double the range once recommended by Lieutenant-General Hawley!

In all three sets of historical trials there are variations in detail as a result of the different circumstances under which the tests were carried out and the size of the target at which the men were actually shooting. Nevertheless, it is very striking how abruptly the accuracy of the smooth-bored flintlock dropped off *beyond* 100yd. In simple terms, because the ball was not normally a perfect fit in the barrel, it tended to career from side to side and would often exit the barrel at an unpredictable angle. This could be prevented to a degree by patching the ball – wrapping it in cloth or cartridge paper to ensure a snug fit – but this was not always practical and was in any case impossible once the barrel started to clog with uneven patches of powder residue.

However, the figures both formal and informal quoted above were obviously obtained under test conditions. There were some dramatic exceptions, such as that 'perfect volley' delivered by Major-General Wolfe's men at Quebec in 1759, but a detailed analysis of a typical cross-section of actual engagements during the Napoleonic Wars demonstrates a much lower level of accuracy than the hit rate of 40–50 per cent or better recorded in those tests. Instead, 'at ranges of 100 yards or less over the full period of an engagement casualties were inflicted by just 5½% of the bullets ordered to be fired' (Hughes 1974: 127, 133).

manner, and then retired into the wood in great disorder: on which we sent our third fire after them, and saw them no more. We advanced cautiously up to the ground which they had quitted, and found several of them killed and wounded … we had but four men killed, and six wounded: and found near forty of them on the spot killed and wounded.

As Parker smugly continued: 'Again the manner of our firing was different from theirs; the *French* at that time fired all by Ranks, which can never do equal execution with our Plattoon-firing, especially when six Plattoons are fired together. This is undoubtedly the best method that has yet been discovered for fighting a Battalion; especially when two Battalions only engage each other' (Parker 1968: 88–89).

In terms of arithmetic, if we suppose both battalions to be of equal strength, as much as one-third of the British muskets were being fired in each volley, as against a quarter of the French ones, even assuming the latter to be drawn up in four ranks rather than the officially prescribed five. Moreover, on the French side the musket's normal tendency to shoot high was also exacerbated by the practice described by Demorinet of commencing firing with the rear rank, who were naturally concerned to avoid blowing the heads off their comrades kneeling in front of them. That particular advantage was of course a theoretical one, and disappeared once the French reduced formation depth from four ranks to three.

Nevertheless, having hit upon what *appeared* to be a highly effective method of fire control, the British Army adhered to it obsessively for the next 50 years. Indeed, it did so to the point where the terms 'volley' and 'platoon' were used interchangeably and officers of quite small detachments could speak of 'firing a platoon' or say that 'we gave them a platoon', rather than a volley. However, successful as platoon firing had been at Malplaquet and other battles in the Duke of Marlborough's day, much of this peacetime obsession actually stemmed from a lack of opportunity for broader training. There were few barracks, and so most British regiments were widely dispersed in billets or on detached duties, or even spending a surprising amount of time simply marching from place

Platoon firing (previous pages)

This plate provides a demonstration of the platoon- or alternate-firing system in its classic form, performed in accordance with David Dundas' *Rules and Regulations* of 1792. Two companies of the 2/1st (Royal) Regiment, which fought against the Republican French at the siege of Toulon in September–December 1793, have been linked together as a division; for fire-control purposes each company is reckoned as a platoon or sub-division, and the two are firing alternately. The platoon standing on the left has just fired a volley and the men are now reloading at their best speed. The other platoon in the division is already loaded and has not only locked its ranks forward, but has recovered its muskets in the 'make ready' position and ideally will wait until its sister platoon has finished reloading before delivering its own volley. Beyond its flank the right-hand platoon of the neighbouring division is actually delivering its fire, but timed slightly behind, as part of a ripple running from the flank of the battalion into the centre. The other two divisions will mirror this ripple by firing in towards the centre from the left flank. The remaining two companies of the regiment, the grenadiers and the light infantry, if not physically detached normally took post behind the flanks as a reserve.

to place. Consequently, they were only brought together to train as a complete battalion for a relatively brief period each year, and in the meantime had little opportunity to practise much more than their basic foot drill and the 'manual exercise', as weapon-handling was termed. This in turn meant that little thought was given to refining the platoon firing system, much less replacing it with something better.

This was unfortunate, because although supposedly an effective means of conducting a static firefight, platoon fire was ill-adapted to stopping a determined assault by men relying instead on their bayonets, or Highland broadswords. To put it simply; a spluttering platoon fire could not kill enough of the attackers fast enough to stop them before they closed those last few critical yards to trigger the fight-or-flight response. Consequently, as early as 1746 we find Lieutenant-General Hawley instructing his troops not to engage in platooning, but to fire by ranks when engaging columns of Highlanders. What was more, notwithstanding his professed disdain for Hawley, James Wolfe advocated much the same thing in the mid-1750s when training his men to counter French column attacks – something which he put to use with devastating effect against the regiments of Béarn and Languedoc on the Plains of Abraham.

The inevitable result of this peacetime obsession with platooning was a dangerous degree of complacency which was badly upset in the 1740s; not just by those fast-moving Jacobite Highlanders, but also by the salutary shock of the battle of Dettingen on 27 June 1743, the first major battle against the French since Malplaquet. There, despite all those years of practice, officers such as the young James Wolfe found to their horror that their supposed ability to control the fire of their men over a sustained period, whether by platooning or by any other means, simply evaporated. Although the British Army again emerged victorious from both experiences, it led Wolfe to introduce Frederick the Great's 'Alternate Firing' while serving as the lieutenant colonel of the 20th Regiment of Foot in 1755:

As the alternate fire by platoons or divisions, or by companies, is the most simple, plain and easy, and used by the best disciplined troops in Europe [i.e. the Prussians], we are at all times to imitate them in that respect, making every platoon receive the word of command, and to make ready and fire from the officer who commands it; because in battle the fire of our artillery and infantry may render it difficult to use any general signals by beat of drum. (Wolfe 1780: 35)

Rather than dividing the battalion into ad hoc divisions and platoons without regard to the existing company organization, the Alternate Firing system was indeed simple and effective. At the time a British infantry battalion comprised just nine companies on the peacetime establishment, one of them being the grenadiers. Before embarking on field exercises or active service, the eight centre or battalion companies were 'levelled'; that is, men were temporarily cross-posted to ensure that each company was approximately the same size. Then, the companies were paired to form the grand divisions in the French manner, as Wolfe went on to explain:

Every grand division consisting of two companies as they now are, is to be told off into three platoons, to be commanded by a captain, a lieutenant, and an ensign, with a serjeant to each [division]; the rest of the officers and non-commissioned officers are to be distributed in the rear to keep compleat the files, to keep the men in their duty, and to supply the places of the officers or serjeants that may be killed or dangerously wounded. (Wolfe 1780: 47)

Notwithstanding official disapproval by the Duke of Cumberland, who was at the time more concerned with enforcing a common system and practice

Grenadiers of the 58th Regiment of Foot are shown in action during the siege of Louisbourg in June–July 1758 in this watercolour by Richard Simkin (1850–1926). Note how both the sergeant, identified by his red-white-red waist sash, and the officer on the right, identified by a crimson silk net sash and lack of heavy accoutrements, are both primarily armed with flintlock muskets and bayonets rather than the archaic halberds and espontoons still being carried by their respective counterparts in the line. Note also that the primary ammunition supply carried in the grenadiers' large cartridge box behind the right hip is supplemented by a smaller belly box containing up to 12 rounds of ready-use ammunition. (Anne S.K. Brown Military Collection, Brown University Library)

throughout the army than with sanctioning deviations from it devised by 'some fertile genius', this modified form of platoon-firing very quickly took hold and officially, if not always in practice, remained the cornerstone of British infantry tactics throughout the life of the flintlock. However, Wolfe also introduced a further refinement. Instead of dividing each two companies into three platoons, his warning orders for the unsuccessful attack on the French lines at Montmorency (31 July 1759) required that the regiments should embark, land and fight *by companies* under their own officers, which as Captain John Knox of the 43rd Regiment of Foot noted, 'afforded the highest satisfaction to the soldiers' (Knox 1914: I.451). No doubt it did; but, more importantly, once the shooting started it was also much easier for the officers to control the fire of their own men.

This new arrangement was then confirmed in the 1764 *Regulations*, when for firing purposes companies were designated as sub-divisions. Although the choice was left to the discretion of the commanding officer as he adjudged the circumstances, volleys were increasingly delivered not by small sub-units, but by divisions, wings or whole battalions.

Loose Files and American Scramble

In any case, the pernicious legacy of firing by sub-units inherited from the old matchlock was soon entirely turned on its head, and again it was in North America, just a few years later during the American Revolutionary War. That conflict was made possible in the first place by the very existence of the flintlock musket, for it was a self-contained weapon system found in many colonial homes, either for militia service or for hunting, or for both. It was accordingly relatively easy to assemble the insurgent forces at the outset, not always at a minute's notice to be sure, but at least with a certain degree of confidence that those willing to take up arms actually possessed those arms in the first place. What the American militias did lack, obviously, was any meaningful training and discipline. This placed them at a considerable disadvantage in the open field, since they could neither manoeuvre effectively nor display the fortitude and tenacity required to conduct a short-range firefight. Instead, in the early days they took to evening the odds by establishing themselves in defensive positions and firing from behind cover. In time the Patriot soldiers of what became designated the Continental Line evolved into very competent regular soldiers, but before that the British Army had itself evolved a new and highly effective tactical doctrine combining both flintlock musket and bayonet.

Even at the best of times a static firefight, as King Louis XIV had declared so long ago, 'involves heavy losses and is never decisive'; and so too, as the dreadful casualties at the battle of Bunker Hill (17 July 1775) demonstrated, did the slow cadenced pace considered essential to preserve the required perfect alignment of the advancing battle line. It did not take long for the British to realize that the most effective way to engage American troops, whether entrenched or out in the open, was to rush them and try to trigger the fight-or-flight reaction. If musketry was required, they might fire by ranks or even by complete battalions, and rapidly follow it up with a bayonet charge. This was delivered not in

The American *Manual Exercise*, very largely based on the familiar British *Regulations* of 1764, as taught to the Continental Army by 'Baron' von Steuben.

column, in the French manner, but in the traditional line formation. In order to accomplish this, it was necessary to relax parade-ground discipline and instead not only adopt a two-deep formation, but tolerate what General William Harcourt would later refer to as 'loose files and American scramble'.

Notwithstanding Major-General David Dundas' attempts to reintroduce the rigidity of 'Prussian' drill and tactics in the early 1790s, the American experience won out and throughout the Napoleonic Wars British practice (as distinct from theory) eschewed platooning or anything resembling it in favour of firing by battalion, or occasionally (according to local circumstances) by wing or by division. Otherwise, practical experience – both in Europe and outside it – only served to confirm the French experience that engaging in a close-range firefight might be all very well when standing on the defensive, but it was likely to stall any attempt to advance, often with fatal consequences. As Lieutenant Andrew Leith Hay, a British staff officer, complained after Wellington's victory at the battle of Salamanca on 22 July 1812:

> The 6th [Division] suffered very much from having been halted when advanced about half way – which is a system that never will answer, the only way is to get at them with the Bayonet, that they [the French] can never stand, but as to firing that they will do as long as you like, and fire much better than we do. (Quoted in Muir 2001: 109)

Rank and file

There was thus, by the beginning of the 19th century, a pronounced but little-remarked convergence in British and French tactical thinking on the use of the flintlock musket, and so too in the manner of conducting a firefight once the advance had stalled. As noted earlier, after firing an initial series of volleys by ranks, French units generally commenced an irregular *feu de billebaude*, in which each man loaded and fired in his own time. This was at first contrasted unfavourably with the fire of British units, who were

49

numerous casualties. It eventually took the Scots Greys to save the day, not by tackling the Jacobites head-on but by rolling up the rebel flank (Reid 2014: 132–34).

Nor was this episode exceptional, for exactly the same was true during the American Revolutionary War. The Patriot regiments might not have been the equal of the British regulars sent against them – at least not at first – but they owed their existence and their eventual victory to the flintlock musket which instantly turned farmers into soldiers. So, too, with the French revolutionary armies in the 1790s, and all the other armies that followed or fought against Napoleon in Spain and Germany and beyond; massed armies, far bigger than those of the 17th and 18th centuries. Some of these citizen armies suffered terrible defeats, of course, but even if one army or another were destroyed, others were very quickly raised to replace them – and all made possible by the universal availability of the simple but effective flintlock musket.

WORLDWIDE IMPACT

Of itself this was impressive enough, but beyond Europe and North America, the impact of the flintlock musket was arguably even greater, and was most dramatically demonstrated in the Far East, first by the French *Compagnie des Indes* and then by Britain's East India Company. Oddly enough, neither the French nor the British trading companies actually set out to conquer India, and indeed their respective boards of directors continually tried to avoid conflict as being expensive in itself and disruptive to trade. However, the 1740s saw the rival companies become increasingly involved in local politics as each sought to improve its position at the expense of the other. Thus at San Thomé, near the southern trading settlement of Pondicherry, on 4 November 1746 a small French army found itself facing a much larger Indian one belonging to the Nawab of the Carnatic. Posted behind the Adyar River, the 10,000-odd Carnatic troops, although individually no doubt as brave as any, were a traditional Indian force as undisciplined and as variously armed with

Sepoys of the 3rd Battalion at Bombay 1773, depicted by Mary Darly (*fl.* 1762–76). Of the three military establishments maintained by Britain's East India Company, that of Bombay was the smallest and least developed in the 18th century, and although published in 1773 this illustration probably provides a fair representation of the Company's earliest uniforms. Essentially, the soldier is dressed entirely in native clothing with the addition of a loose red jacket on top, but he is rather more clearly identified as a soldier by his flintlock musket and bayonet and by the obvious fact that he has been trained by a European drillmaster. His accoutrements, if accurately depicted, appear odd and may represent some kind of powder flask and bullet bag, but it is very difficult to say. Note that the right-hand figure also appears to be carrying a cane, perhaps as a non-lethal weapon for use against civilians. (Anne S.K. Brown Military Collection, Brown University Library)

matchlock muskets, bows, pikes, swords and other edged weapons as any army of the Eighty Years' War in the Netherlands or the Thirty Years' War in Germany. Most of the *Compagnie des Indes* forces opposing them were similarly equipped local mercenaries, but among them there were 350 European soldiers. There was nothing special about these soldiers; they were not well-trained or disciplined veterans, but rather the usual collection of the desperate and the criminal, and a few genuine adventurers, most of whom had left their home country for their country's good. However, unlike their opponents, all of them were armed with flintlocks and bayonets.

Finding the Nawab's men showing no immediate inclination to advance, the Swiss officer who commanded the *Compagnie* troops, Major Louis Paradis, gallantly decided to attack. With those 350 Frenchmen at his back, Paradis splashed straight across the river, had them fire a single volley and then immediately led them forward again with fixed bayonets. To the astonishment of all, he won a stunning victory as the Nawab's men, reeling from that volley and thoroughly intimidated by the bayonet charge that followed, scattered and fled in confusion. Paradis, as the historian Sir John Fortescue memorably wrote, had 'showed us the secret of how to conquer India' – with flintlock musket and bayonet. The lesson was quickly taken to heart, and in what amounted to a rerun of Paradis' victory just over ten years later it was the East India Company's turn. At Plassey on 23 June 1757, a similarly outnumbered British force led by Colonel Robert Clive stormed forward with musket and bayonet and utterly defeated the Nawab of Bengal in a battle which traditionally marks the beginning of the British Empire.

In this detail from a depiction by Henry Martens (1790–1868) of the battle of Gujrat (or Goojerat), 21 February 1849, during the Second Anglo-Sikh War, the trio of sepoys look very different from their Bombay counterparts of nearly a century before and have clearly been completely assimilated into the European military system. Their uniforms are all but identical to those worn by the East India Company's European troops and British regulars, and only their dark-skinned features and facial hair identify them as Indians. Just as importantly, and in contrast to the ambiguity as to the type of accoutrements carried by their Bombay forebears in the Mary Darly print of 1773, these men are carrying standard European-pattern belts and pouches. (Anne S.K. Brown Military Collection, Brown University Library)

Although the decisive attack was carried out by Europeans, as many as two-thirds of Clive's troops at Plassey were *sepoys* – locally recruited Indian soldiers tentatively trained and equipped in the European manner with flintlocks and bayonets. Such was the success of this experiment that over the next 100 years the East India Company's armies became overwhelmingly comprised of *sepoy* units. Significantly, the local rulers were themselves equally capable of learning the lessons of San Thomé and Plassey. Consequently, the Company's troops very soon found themselves fighting against other equally well-equipped *sepoys* organized and trained for those native princes by European mercenaries. The Mahrattas, who were defeated with considerable difficulty during a series of wars in southern India during the early 1800s, were a notable example, but more formidable still was the *Khalsa* or Sikh army in the north. The two wars which the East India Company fought against the Sikhs in the 1840s were to all intents and purposes brutal and bloody European-style conflicts translated to the heat and dust of India. Indeed, had it not been for political infighting amongst the Sikh leadership, the Company might have been badly defeated – and even then victory was a very close-run thing indeed.

Nor did it end there. By the middle of the 19th century, European methods of warfare based around the flintlock musket and its bayonet had spread around and dominated the world except in the closed empires of China and Japan, and even they would have substantially assimilated them before the century was out. European artillery also played a part in this transformation, of course, but it was the flintlock musket which initiated the process.

THE RISE OF LIGHT INFANTRY

Thus far, European armies still generally held to the legacy of Prince Johan of Nassau and his drill books, which instilled the immutable principle that, just as in classical times, constant drill and the inculcation of strict discipline were absolutely necessary to create soldiers. The problem thereby was that while Frederick the Great's Prussian Guards undoubtedly represented the perfection of that ideal, they were a very expensive commodity indeed. There is an exact parallel here with the British Army of 1914, which was small – perhaps contemptibly small – but yet reckoned to be the most professional in the world. Nevertheless, within four desperate months of fighting, culminating in the First Battle of Ypres in October–November 1914, it had had been all but destroyed; and those who replaced them were very different in character. Exactly the same had been true of those Prussian, Hanoverian and British regulars, so ferociously trained in platoon firing before the Seven Years' War (1754–63) and equally quick to waste away once it began.

It was at this point that the flintlock musket came into its own, by making it possible to raise not just replacement drafts for veteran units, but also to create and deploy whole new regiments very quickly. It was the old story of those Jacobite rebels at Sheriffmuir in 1715, and indeed those earlier French infantrymen deplored by Louvois. Given a flintlock musket and a bayonet, only a modicum of training sufficed to turn raw recruits into reasonably effective soldiers. More importantly, at the same time, and at first sight paradoxically, the flintlock also brought about an utterly fundamental change in the very nature of soldiering; one which was seemingly totally at odds with the rigid discipline required to turn an infantry battalion into what Frederick the Great approvingly described as a 'moving battery'.

Ironically, Frederick himself was one of the first to fall foul of this revolution. In 1740 he had invaded the Austrian Habsburg possession of Silesia, opportunistically hoping to profit from the disputed Imperial succession. Unable to rely upon the German states, the young Empress Maria Theresa turned to her quite separate kingdom of Hungary for assistance. Not only did the Hungarian Army contribute hussars and regular infantry, but at the time the kingdom also included the Balkan provinces which formed a volatile frontier with the Turkish empire, and so there also appeared hordes of irregular cavalry and infantry, promiscuously referred to as *Crabbates* (Croats) and *Pandours*.

These wild *Grenztruppen* (frontier troops) knew nothing of discipline, but all of them were armed with flintlock muskets, and instead of standing in a rigid battle line and marching at a regulated pace, they moved and fired individually as part of a loose cloud of skirmishers. In the open they were easily ridden down by cavalry or brushed aside by regular infantry, and were consequently prone to running away to avoid either. In close country, however, whether wooded or lined with hedges or cluttered with villages and other settlements, it was a very different matter. There they made sufficient nuisance of themselves to compel their opponents to reciprocate by raising their own irregular units of 'light infantry'. According to the Prussian military theorist and reformer Gerhard von Scharnhorst:

> Immediately after the battle of Mollwitz, where [Frederick] experienced and recognised his lack of such units, he made it his first task to strengthen his army with light troops. By the Second Silesian War he was able to oppose the Austrians with a relatively equal force. His example was followed by the French, the Hanoverians and the Saxons, all of whom founded units of this branch of the service. Nevertheless the proportion of these troops to line formations remained extremely small ... (Quoted in Gates 1987: 11, 24)

Frederick had done so grudgingly and with obvious distaste, characterizing his own *Frei-bataillone* as being comprised of 'Adventurers, deserters and vagabonds who are distinguished from the regular infantry only by the lack of what made the infantry strong, namely, discipline' (quoted in Gates 1987: 24). In complete contrast, Frederick's then allies, the French, took a rather different view of the matter. They did not quite share his concern over maintaining a rigid discipline and enthusiastically embraced the individualism required of flintlock-armed light infantrymen. The reluctance of Louvois and his master King Louis XIV to embrace the

Brisbane, why stand here while the brigade gets cut up? Form line, and send out the 45th skirmishing.' Two companies being left with the colours, the rest of us ascended the hill, to be received in such a manner as I had never before experienced. We were but a skirmishing line opposed to a dense column supported by artillery and cavalry. The bullets flew thick as hail, thirteen men of my company alone fell within a few yards of me on the brow of the hill. Notwithstanding we pressed on, and the enemy after dreadful carnage gave way, and left us in possession of a ditch, which we held until the brigade came up in line. We then gave three cheers, charged the enemy's light troops, and drove them from another ditch parallel with the one we had just taken. Having repeatedly charged, and been charged in turn, we got on the height, from which we had a complete view of the dark masses of the enemy in column, one of which was moving against us, the officers hat in hand waving on the men in advance. By this time we were greatly diminished – nearly half down or disabled – and might have given way, if a staff officer had not come up at the critical moment and encouraged us to hold our ground, as we should be relieved in a minute. (Quoted in Oman 1930: VII.359–60)

The 45th Regiment of Foot was an ordinary regiment of the line, not a light-infantry corps, and so it would be difficult to find a more dramatic contrast to Robert Parker's account of the 18th Regiment of Foot and its platoon firing at Malplaquet just over a century earlier.

INDIVIDUAL FIRE

At the same time, the process was going still further with a steadily increasing emphasis on individual aimed fire. Following up that earlier order, another circular in 1801 recommended that 'Individuals … [should

The use of aimed fire, rather than simply levelling, is very clearly depicted in Windham's *A Plan of Discipline, Composed for the Use of the Militia of the County of Norfolk*, itself based on French practice.

71

be] occasionally detached and instructed how to act as Flankers, and as skirmishers in attacking, or repelling those of the Enemy; ... accustomed not to fire, but when they have a good Mark and Aim' (quoted in Gates 1987: 143). It is worth emphasizing once again that the 'flankers' or 'marksmen' referred to were not members of the regimental light companies, but were instead drawn from the ordinary battalion companies.

Individually aimed fire *à tirailleur* was by no means an innovation, of course, but rather a belated acknowledgement of best practice originating in those cheap-and-cheerful *chasseur* units and in the ranger units in North America. Notwithstanding the test results quoted in the previous chapter, in practical terms the accuracy of the flintlock musket was in fact perfectly adequate and fit for that purpose. Indeed, it was probably a good deal more accurate than is generally acknowledged, the real problem being not the weapon itself but how it was actually handled. If this at first appears paradoxical in light of those results, it is important once again to appreciate that volley firing was not conducive to good marksmanship. As the Comte de Guibert wrote:

Those Prussian battalions, so famously esteemed for their order and execution, are those whose fire is less galling; their first discharge has precision and effect because this first shot is loaded out of action, and done with more attention and regularity; but afterwards in the heat and confusion of an engagement, they load in haste, and are inattentive to the well ramming of their charges. They are told that the great perfection of their exercise consists in making the most fires in a minute; no wonder then if they pay such little attention to the levelling of their pieces. Busied with this imaginary effect of celerity, at the expense of teaching the true position of adjusting the aim, they have acquired no proper idea of the true theory of their shot or fire. (Guibert 1781: I.162–63)

The same alas was no doubt true of Richard Parker's men at Malplaquet, who it will be recalled had only fired that first shot from each platoon. On the other hand, encouraging a soldier to shoot as an individual rather than as part of a platoon meant he was able to do so in the manner best suited to the circumstances. In 1715 John, Master of Sinclair, recorded how during a rather tense stand-off with some Highlanders, 'they pretended they did not understand me and most cockt their pieces, and presented, to shoot me, and some lay doun on their bellies to take the better aime' (Sinclair 1858: 101). It is interesting to find such an early reference to lying down to take better aim, but lying down or otherwise supporting a musket while taking careful aim was always going to produce better results than those recorded in the formal trials of volley fire delivered by men standing rigidly upright. Interestingly, the eccentric Colonel George Hanger bombastically declared in 1808 that:

> A soldier's musket, if not exceedingly badly bored, and *very crooked, as many are*, will strike the figure of a man at 80 yards, it may even at 100 yards; but a soldier *must be very unfortunate indeed* who shall be wounded by a *common musket* at 150 yards, PROVIDED HIS ANTAGONIST AIMS AT HIM; and as to firing at a man at 200 yards with a common musket, you may just as well fire at the moon, and have as much hopes of hitting your object. I do maintain … that NO MAN WAS EVER KILLED AT 200 YARDS by a common soldier's musket, by the person who aimed at him. (Quoted in Gates 1987: 139)

Notwithstanding the tone of his remarks, Colonel Hanger, a noted sportsman, was clearly confident that at ranges up to 100yd it was perfectly feasible to hit a man-sized target with a smooth-bored flintlock musket providing a proper aim was taken. Indeed, in fighting at close quarters, within and sometimes well within that optimal 100yd envelope, the soldier's own ability to hit a given target was – and still is – far more important than the theoretical accuracy of the weapon itself. As to shooting beyond that range, the evident falling-off in accuracy after 100yd might not have been as critical in tactical terms as it first appears. Significantly, after more than a century of equipping soldiers with long-barrelled rifles sighted up to 1,000m (1,094yd) or more, modern armies have now turned to short-barrelled assault weapons in response to the realization that – notwithstanding technological advances – most infantry combats still take place within that 100yd envelope.

What is more, when engaged at such a short distance there was often no time to aim properly, and it was necessary to resort to snap shooting. At close range, say within 25yd, snap shooting is actually a surprisingly

OPPOSITE In a foretaste of modern practice, this American officer carries a fusil or musket and bayonet. The 'C.C.' on his cartridge box probably stands for Continental Congress.

This depiction of the battle of Orthez on 27 February 1814 by William Heath (1795–1840) is conventional in composition and to a large extent fanciful, but it does provide a basic representation of the difficult ridge-top position which the 45th Regiment of Foot had to assault not in conventional close order, but in a dispersed firing line as skirmishers. Had he witnessed it, David Dundas would no doubt have been horrified. (Anne S.K. Brown Military Collection, Brown University Library)

effective technique which essentially amounts to relying on hand-eye co-ordination, or pointing and shooting in other words, rather than trying to squint uncertainly along a wavering barrel. Colonel Kenneth Mackenzie, who trained the British Army's regular light-infantry regiments for Sir John Moore, explained it thus:

> A soldier who from habit, can bring his firelock in a line with the object he is looking at, has a good chance of hitting the Enemy … even in the hurry and confusion of action because he is so instructed, that his firelock mechanically comes … in a direct line with the object he is looking at … for the eye naturally directs the hand to the object it is looking at. (Quoted in Gates 1987: 147)

And so they went forward carrying their flintlocks, with each man picking his own target; not just the regimental *chasseur* or *tirailleur* or light companies, or even for that matter the vaunted riflemen; not specialists but ordinary soldiers, first forming an increasingly heavy screen for the battalions behind and then, like the 45th Regiment of Foot at Orthez, replacing them and thus establishing the foundation of modern infantry tactics.

CONCLUSION

The success of the flintlock musket may be gauged not just by its iconic status and its long-term impact on the conduct of warfare, but also by the fact that in the immediate term it was upgraded rather than replaced. In 1806, the Reverend Alexander Forsyth successfully demonstrated a prototype percussion lock. Under this new system the clamp or cock was replaced by a hammer and the priming pan and frizzen by a tube filled with powdered fulminate of mercury, which detonated on being struck and flashed through the touch-hole to ignite the powder charge in the barrel.

Further development was required to refine the initial design for military use, by replacing the powdered fulminate with a paste varnished

After dominating battlefields for two centuries, thanks to a combination of Forsyth's percussion system and the Minié ball the development of the flintlock reached its culmination in the Pattern 1853 Enfield rifle-musket – a reproduction weapon is shown here – only for it to be rendered obsolete within a decade by breech-loaders. Mechanically, the percussion lock was similar to the flintlock, with the cock simply being replaced by a hammer. The priming pan and frizzen, however, were replaced by a nipple on which a copper cap was placed, which when struck flashed a flame to the powder charge in the barrel.

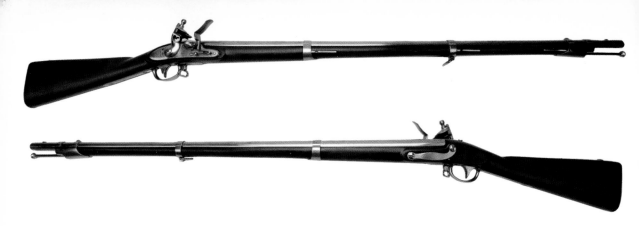

ABOVE The US 1816 Pattern Springfield illustrated here was, like its predecessor, a direct copy of a French Charleville-type weapon, in this case the ubiquitous Modèle 1777 which had served Napoleon and his allies so well. At first glance the two are identical and indeed largely distinguished by their respective markings. This effectively served as the US Army's standard pattern musket until the adoption of the percussion system and even then soldiered on, sometimes but not always converted to percussion, up to the early years of the American Civil War. 1816 Pattern muskets were supplied in some numbers to the rebels in Texas in 1836 and afterwards the short-lived Republic of Texas adopted it as the standard firearm for its regular army. (NRA Museums, NRAmuseums.com)

OPPOSITE Among the last users of the flintlock musket in combat were the Americans, in the US–Mexican War of 1846–48. A militiaman of the Cleveland Grays is depicted in this pencil-and-watercolour sketch by Jarvis Frary Hanks (1799–1853). (Anne S.K. Brown Military Collection, Brown University Library)

to a copper wafer or cap, but in November 1831 the first contract was placed for converting 200 India Pattern flintlocks to a percussion system. Extensive testing followed, paralleled on the Continent and in North America, and in 1836 the first large-scale trials followed, culminating in the Pattern 1838 musket, set up from the beginning with a percussion lock. In parallel, a Pattern 1839 musket was also approved to utilize existing stocks of parts originally intended for setting up flintlocks. Both were then followed by the 1842 pattern, but to all intents and purposes all three patterns were essentially flintlock muskets fitted with improved locks, and were handled and employed exactly as before.

It was much the same in the United States of America, where not only were thousands of 1816 and 1822 Pattern flintlocks converted to the percussion system, but some even survived unconverted until the American Civil War in the 1860s. For lack of anything better, thousands were issued to Confederate units early in the war, especially in the heartland states, and some even survived to the war's end in the hands of home guard units. Similarly, the French Army adopted its own pattern percussion musket in 1840, but largely relied on flintlock conversions until the invention of the Minié ball opened the way for the development of the rifle-musket as a general-issue weapon rather than one for specialists. The Minié ball was a slightly undersized conidial bullet with a hollow base. On being fired, a wood or clay plug in the base then forced the lower part of the bullet into the rifling. It could therefore be loaded just as quickly and easily as a conventional smooth-bored musket, but was obviously capable of far greater accuracy and a longer range.

The Duke of Wellington, still commander-in-chief of the British Army at the time, approved the introduction of a Minié rifle for general issue, but insisted that it should be referred to as a rifle-musket, not a rifle, as he wished to preserve the tactical distinction between infantry of the line and specialist sharpshooters. Hence the term rifle-musket, as epitomized by the famous Pattern 1853 Enfield which was fired using a percussion lock and had a rifled barrel, but which arguably represented the culmination of 200 years of the flintlock musket.

There was also one last curious survival. As late as World War I, by which time the British Army had progressed to the Lee Enfield bolt-action rifle with its ten-round magazine, the term musketry was still synonymous with the crackle and roar of small-arms fire.

GLOSSARY

BAYONET: Blade affixed to the muzzle of a musket; originally a dagger plugged directly into the bore but latterly of triangular section offset from the barrel by means of an external socket.

BRIDLE: Keeper plate within lock mechanism.

CARBINE: Lightweight musket used by cavalrymen, artillery crews and some light infantry; latterly a short-barrelled weapon, but not invariably so.

COCK: External clamp which holds the flint; originally swan-necked, but latterly incorporating a reinforcing ring.

DOG: Safety catch.

FIRELOCK: Musket incorporating an intrinsic ignition mechanism, as distinct from a matchlock, which required an external means of igniting the priming charge.

FLINT: Shard of quartz, knapped or shaped by striking flakes off to create a wedge shape with a sharp cutting edge which would strike sparks off hardened surfaces such as steel.

FRIZZEN: Hardened steel plate (in North American usage, a hammer) off which sparks are struck by the flint to ignite the priming charge.

FUSIL: Light musket; originally a French term and sometimes rendered phonetically in English as 'fusee'.

HAMMER: See frizzen; not to be confused with the hammer of a percussion lock.

LOCKPLATE: Metal plate to which all of lock components are attached.

NOSECAP: Metal cap, strengthening the forend of the stock at the interface with the fixed bayonet.

PLATOON: Infantry sub-unit used for fire-control purposes, but also slang for a volley.

PRIMING CHARGE: Small quantity of gunpowder used to ignite the propellant charge.

PRIMING PAN: Small pan external to the musket barrel which contained the priming charge used to ignite the propellant inside the barrel. A 'flash in the pan' is a term denoting a failure of the priming charge to ignite the propellant.

SEAR: Linking piece between trigger and tumbler.

SIDENAILS: Two transverse screw-headed bolts passing through the stock to secure the lock.

SIDEPLATE: Small metal plate, usually of cast brass let into the stock on the reverse side to the lock to serve as an anchor for the sidenails.

SLING: Leather strap intended to allow the flintlock musket to be carried hands-free.

SNAPHAUNCE: Early form of flintlock mechanism.

STEEL: See frizzen.

TUMBLER: Lock component to which the cock (or, in percussion system, hammer) is attached.

BIBLIOGRAPHY

Bailey, D.W. (1986). *British Military Longarms 1715–1865*. London: Arms & Armour.

Blackmore, H.L. (1994). *British Military Firearms 1650–1850*. London: Greenhill.

Chandler, David (1976). *The Art of War in the Age of Marlborough*. London: Batsford.

Dundas, David (1792). *Rules and Regulations for the Formations, Field Exercise and Movements of His Majesty's Forces*. London: War Office.

Gates, David (1987). *The British Light Infantry Arm c.1790–1815*. London: Batsford.

Guderian, Heinz (2000). *Panzer Leader*. London: Penguin. Originally published in 1950.

Guibert, Comte de (1781), trans. Lieutenant Douglas. *General Essay of Tactics*. London: J. Millan. Originally published in 1772.

Hardin, Stephen (1994). *Texian Iliad: A military history of the Texas Revolution*. Austin, TX: University of Texas Press.

Houlding, J.A. (1988). *French Arms Drill of the 18th Century*. Bloomfield, IN: Museum Restoration Service.

Hughes, B.P. (1974). *Firepower: Weapons effectiveness on the battlefield 1630–1850*. London: Arms & Armour.

Knox, John (1914–16). *An Historical Journal of the Campaigns in North America*. Toronto: Champlain Society.

Lawson, C.C.P. (1961). *History of the Uniforms of the British Army Vol. III*. London: Norman Military Publications.

Muir, Rory (2001). *Salamanca 1812*. New Haven, CT & London: Yale University Press.

Oman, Charles (1902–30). *History of the Peninsular War*. 7 vols. Oxford: Clarendon Press.

Parker, Robert, ed. D. Chandler (1968). *Memories of the Most Memorable Military Transactions*. London: Longman.

Peterkin, Ernest (1989). *The Exercise of Arms in the Continental Infantry*. Bloomfield, IN: Museum Restoration Service.

Reid, Stuart (2014). *Sheriffmuir 1715*. Barnsley: Frontline.

Saxe, Maurice de, ed. T.R. Philips (1944). *Reveries on the Art of War*. Harrisburg, PA: Military Service Publishing Company. Originally published in 1757, but probably written or dictated in December 1732.

Sinclair, John (1858). *Memoirs of the Insurrection in Scotland in 1715*. Edinburgh: Abbotsford Club.

Stewart of Garth, David (1822). *Sketches of the Character, manners and present state of the Highlanders of Scotland*. 2 vols. Edinburgh: Constable.

Terry, Charles Sandford (1917). *Papers Relating to the Army of the Solemn League and Covenant, 1643–1647. Volume 1*. Edinburgh: Scottish History Society.

Tomasson, K. & Buist, F. (1967). *Battles of the '45*. London: Batsford.

Walker, Edward (1705). *Historical Works: Brief Memorials of the Unfortunate Success of His Majesty's Army and Affairs in the Year 1645*. London: publisher not known.

Wilkinson, Henry (1841). *Engines of War: or, Historical and Experimental Observations ...* London: Longman, Orme, Brown, Green, and Longmans.

Willson, Beckles (1909). *The Life and Letters of James Wolfe*. London: William Heinemann.

Wolfe, James (1780). *General Wolfe's INSTRUCTIONS to Young Officers*. London: J. Millan.

INDEX

Figures in **bold** refer to illustrations.